Building Generational Wealth

Leaving a Legacy for Your Loved Ones

Andrew Galowey

Copyright © [Andrew Galowey] [2024]. All rights reserved. No part of this publication may be reproduced, distributed, or transmitted in any form or by any means, including photocopying, recording, or other electronic or mechanical methods, without the prior written permission of the publisher, except in the case of brief quotations embodied in critical reviews and certain other noncommercial uses permitted by copyright law.

Table Of Contents

Introduction

Chapter 1: Determining Generational Wealth and Creating Your Legacy Plan

Chapter 2: The Cornerstones: Wills and Trusts—Tools for Secure Distribution

Chapter 3: Planning for the Future: Reducing Taxes and Increasing Benefits

Chapter 4: Empowering Your Heirs: Choosing Beneficiaries and Developing Responsible Stewardship

Chapter 5: Creating a Legacy Beyond Money: Education Funding and Other Strategies

Conclusion

Introduction

Have you ever pondered how to leave a lasting impression on your family's future? Building generational wealth is more than just acquiring money; it is about leaving a legacy that empowers and uplifts your loved ones for future generations. In "Building Generational Wealth: Leaving a Legacy for Your Loved Ones," you'll learn how to navigate the world of estate planning and asset transfer. Whether you're just getting started with your finances or wanting to improve an existing plan, this book will walk you through the process of making wills and trusts, lowering estate taxes, selecting beneficiaries, and building financial vehicles to safeguard your family's security and prosperity. Let's go on this adventure together and discover the keys of leaving a legacy that lasts generations.

Chapter 1: Determining Generational Wealth and Creating Your Legacy Plan

Consider a bright summer evening, with laughter booming around the home as your grandkids play. You reminisce with your spouse about the life you've created together, the obstacles you've faced, and the aspirations you've fulfilled. However, when you consider a legacy that will last beyond your lifetime, you have a greater feeling of fulfillment. This is the core of developing generational wealth: laying a financial foundation that will empower and elevate your loved ones for future generations.

This book isn't only about saving money. It is about adopting a proactive approach to ensuring that your hard-earned assets are successfully dispersed and continue to benefit your family long after you die. It's about leaving a legacy that represents your beliefs, promotes financial stability, and allows future generations to prosper.

Breaking the Cycle: From Accumulation to Legac

Many of us grow raised with an emphasis on financial security. We work hard, strive for financial stability, and want to offer a pleasant lifestyle for ourselves and our family. However, establishing generational wealth extends beyond the initial accumulation period. It necessitates a change in perspective, from merely accumulating resources to carefully planning their distribution and long-term effect.

Consider households you know in whom money seems to disappear within a generation or two. Perhaps excessive spending or a lack of financial knowledge contributed to its decline. Building generational wealth entails breaking the pattern by devising a strategy that promotes responsible stewardship and ensures your legacy remains.

Defining Your Legacy: What Values Do You Want to Pass On?

The basis of your legacy strategy goes beyond financial assets. It is about the ideals you hold dear and the ideas you want to inculcate in future generations. Do you appreciate education and want to make sure your grandkids have access to higher learning opportunities? Is financial independence essential to you, and do you want to help your successors make wise financial decisions?

Understanding your basic principles is the foundation for creating a meaningful legacy strategy. It influences how you share money and the methods you employ to attain your objectives. For example, if you value financial responsibility, you can consider forming trusts with particular access requirements.

Creating Your Vision: Goals and Aspirations

Building generational wealth is a continuous effort that starts with a clear goal. Reflect on your legacy objectives and desires. What does financial stability mean for future generations? Do you imagine your family buying a vacation property, supporting a particular cause, or just having the flexibility to follow their interests?

Once you've identified your broad objectives, break them down into manageable stages. This might include calculating the amount of money you want to transfer, assessing your present assets and obligations, and investigating estate planning options such as wills and trusts.

The Roadmap to Success: Creating Your Legacy Plan

This book will be a valuable resource as you work to generate generational wealth. In the next chapters, we will go further into estate planning tools and methods, tax reduction tactics, and how to identify and empower responsible beneficiaries. We'll help you create wills and trusts, set up educational funds, and make educated judgments regarding tax consequences.

By the conclusion of this trip, you'll have the knowledge and confidence to build a complete legacy plan that represents your vision, protects your assets, and provides a foundation for future generations to thrive. Remember, creating generational wealth is a marathon, not a sprint. Take it one step at a time, celebrate your accomplishments, and enjoy the pleasure of creating a legacy that will have a long-lasting influence on your loved ones.

Chapter 2: The Cornerstones: Wills and Trusts—Tools for Secure Distribution

Consider the following scenario: You've worked relentlessly your whole life to build riches. You have a loving family and a clear plan for your legacy. What happens if you die without a plan in place? Wills and trusts are important instruments for ensuring that your desires are carried out and your assets are dispersed as you plan.

Wills: The Bedrock of Estate Planning

A will is a basic legal document that expresses your desires about the transfer of your possessions after your death. It permits you to designate an executor, who will be in charge of administering your estate and following out the directions included in the will.

Here's a summary of some important aspects of a will:

- Beneficiary Designation: This determines who will inherit your assets, which may include property, bank accounts, and personal things.
- Guardianship Designation: If you have small children, you may use your will to choose a guardian who will look after them in your absence.
- specified Bequests: In your will, you may leave specified things or sums of money to certain people or charity.

Advantages of Wills:

Wills are often simpler and less costly to form than trusts. You may locate internet resources or work with an attorney to create one.

- Flexibility: You may simply make revisions to your will during your life to reflect changes in your circumstances or desires.

Disadvantages of Wills

- Wills go through probate, which is a time-consuming and public judicial procedure. This might cause delays in wealth distribution and perhaps higher legal expenses.
- Wills provide only limited control since they are only effective after your death. They do not have procedures for managing your assets while you are alive or disabled.

Trusts: Taking Control and avoiding Probate

A trust is a legal structure in which you transfer ownership of assets (the trust corpus) to a trustee, who administers those assets for the benefit of the beneficiaries you choose. Trusts have various benefits over wills.

- Avoiding Probate: Assets maintained in a properly constituted trust are often

not probated, saving your beneficiaries time and money.
- Management and Control: You may describe how the trust assets are handled and dispersed, including the terms under which beneficiaries get their inheritance.
- Incapacity Planning: Create a living trust to handle your assets even if you become incapacitated during your lifetime.

Types of Trusts for Different Needs:

There are many sorts of trusts, each tailored to a unique situation:

- Revocable Living Trust: Allows you to keep control of your assets while you are alive and make modifications to the trust as necessary.
- Irrevocable Trust: Assets held in this trust are normally beyond your control and cannot be reclaimed. However,

irrevocable trusts may provide tax advantages.

A Special Needs Trust protects assets for a disabled beneficiary, allowing them to continue receiving government assistance.

Choosing the Right Tool: Wills Versus Trusts

The selection between a will and a trust is based on your specific circumstances and desires. This is a brief guide:

A will may sufficient if you have a reasonably basic estate and your distribution preferences are clear.
Consider a trust if you have a large estate, small children, or want to avoid probate while maintaining control over asset management.

Wills and trusts are essential instruments for ensuring that your possessions are transferred how you intend. Understanding their differences and benefits allows you to choose the best tool for your requirements. Consulting with an estate planning attorney may assist you in developing a thorough plan that represents your unique circumstances and provides a solid foundation for your family's future.

Chapter 3: Planning for the Future: Reducing Taxes and Increasing Benefits

Building generational wealth is more than simply acquiring assets; it is also about ensuring that the greatest amount of money reaches your loved ones. Unfortunately, estate taxes may greatly reduce the value of your estate. This chapter goes at options for reducing taxes and increasing wealth transfer to future generations.

Understanding The Estate Tax Landscape

The federal estate tax applies to estates that surpass a specific threshold, which is presently set relatively high (more than $12.9 million for people in 2024). However, other states impose their own estate taxes with lower limits. When preparing your legacy, it is critical to understand the ramifications of both federal and state estate taxes.

Tax minimization strategies:

While estate taxes may seem onerous, a few measures might help you reduce their effect.

- Use the Lifetime give Exemption: The IRS permits you to give a set amount of money (currently $17,000 per person in 2024) each year without paying gift taxes. You may take advantage of this exemption by making targeted gifts during your life, thereby lowering the taxable value of your estate.

- Marital Deduction: For married couples, assets bequeathed to the surviving spouse are usually excluded from estate taxes. This permits one spouse to die away without having their estate taxed, possibly increasing the total amount passed to future generations.

- Charitable Giving: Donations to qualifying charity provide considerable tax savings. You may deduct charitable gifts from your taxable estate, which lowers your total tax burden. Consider creating charitable trusts to give a piece of your inheritance to causes you care about while reducing your tax obligation.

Life Insurance Strategy:

Life insurance may be an effective instrument for increasing generational wealth. By identifying your recipients as policyholders, you may establish a tax-efficient manner to transfer money. The death benefit is paid directly to your beneficiaries and is often tax-free. This might give them with a large cash buffer after your death.

Leveraging Trusts for Tax Efficiency:

Certain forms of trusts provide specific tax benefits.

- Grantor Retained Annuity Trust (GRAT): You transfer assets to a GRAT while keeping the right to receive an annuity payment for a fixed duration. The remaining assets in the trust are subsequently transferred to your beneficiaries, maybe at a lower taxable value.
- You donate assets to a charitable remainder trust (CRT), which provides income to you or another recipient for a specified amount of time. When the trust is terminated, the residual assets are transferred to a selected charity. You obtain a charitable deduction for the present value of the leftover interest paid to the charity, while your recipients receive income for a certain length of time.

Planning for the unexpected:

Life may be unpredictable. While reducing estate taxes is vital, your first goal should be to ensure that your loved ones are cared for in any circumstance. This may involve:

- Adequate Life Insurance: Make sure your life insurance policy is enough to satisfy your family's immediate financial requirements after you die.
- Disability Planning: Consider purchasing disability insurance to preserve your income and keep your financial plan on track even if you become handicapped.

Creating generational wealth requires a deliberate and purposeful strategy. Understanding estate tax rules and implementing available solutions such as lifelong giving, the marriage deduction, and different trust structures may help you reduce the tax burden on your estate while ensuring your legacy lives on. Remember, the aim is to maximize the wealth you pass to your loved ones while still giving them with the financial stability they deserve. Consulting with an estate planning attorney and a tax specialist may assist you in developing a personalized strategy that maximizes your position while minimizing tax repercussions.

Chapter 4: Empowering Your Heirs: Choosing Beneficiaries and Developing Responsible Stewardship

Building generational wealth entails more than just amassing assets and reducing taxes. It is about ensuring that those assets are handed on to responsible people who will utilize them properly and expand on your legacy. This chapter goes into the critical process of selecting beneficiaries and instilling appropriate financial management in future generations.

Selecting Beneficiaries: Beyond Blood Ties

While your children and spouse are typically obvious benefactors, it is important to consider factors other than family connections while making these selections. Here are some important considerations to consider.

- Maturity and Responsibility: Are your recipients financially responsible and capable of handling substantial assets? Think about their financial background, spending patterns, and general attitude to money management.
- Age and Life Stage: Leaving a significant bequest to a young adult may not be the wisest choice. Consider creating trusts that allow cash to be accessed at specified ages or milestones.
- Understanding Their Values: Are your beneficiaries' values consistent with your own? If you value responsible stewardship and long-term wealth growth, you may wish to examine systems that promote sensible financial decision-making.

Beyond Children: Alternative Beneficiaries

Your legacy strategy does not have to be limited to immediate relatives. Consider the following options:

- grandkids or Other Loved Ones: You may specify inheritances for grandkids or other cherished family members.
- Education Funds: Create educational trusts to guarantee that future generations may pursue their academic goals.
- Charitable Giving: Leave a percentage of your estate to organizations or causes that you love and wish to see grow for future generations.

Fostering Financial Literacy and Responsible Stewardship

Empowering your heirs extends beyond merely passing riches. Provide them with the information and skills required to handle their funds appropriately. Here are a few strategies:

- Open Communication: Discuss your legacy strategy with your recipients. Explain your values and preferences for the assets they will get.
- Financial Education: Help your beneficiaries achieve good financial literacy. Encourage their education in investing, budgeting, and good financial planning.
- Professional Advice: Consider enlisting a financial counselor or wealth manager in the process. They may provide continuous advice and help to your heirs as they handle their inherited assets.

Structure Your Plan for Responsible Management

Several estate planning instruments may assist guarantee appropriate asset management.

- Conditional Trusts: Create trusts that distribute inheritances gradually or based on particular milestones, such as finishing school or reaching a certain age.
- Spendthrift Provisions: These rules in trusts prevent beneficiaries from wasting assets and maintain long-term financial stability.
- Professional Fiduciary: Appoint a trustworthy person or organization (a fiduciary) to handle trust assets. This adds an extra degree of responsibility and promotes smart management.

Addressing blended families and potential conflict

Blended families bring distinct estate planning concerns. Clear communication and equitable distribution may assist to reduce possible conflict. To negotiate these issues, consider contacting an estate planning attorney.

Choosing beneficiaries and encouraging ethical management are critical components of creating generational wealth. You can ensure your legacy goes beyond simply transferring assets by carefully selecting heirs who share your values, providing them with financial literacy, and structuring your plan for responsible management. This will lay the groundwork for future generations' financial security and prosperity. Open communication, continual education, and well developed legal instruments are essential for ensuring that your legacy goal becomes a lasting reality.

Chapter 5: Creating a Legacy Beyond Money: Education Funding and Other Strategies

Building generational wealth is more than simply amassing financial assets. It is about leaving a lasting impression on your family and the world around you. This chapter delves into nontraditional wealth transfer options, with an emphasis on education funds, family enterprises, and charity giving as ways to define your legacy and empower future generations.

Investing in Education: A Springboard to Success

Education is an essential component of social mobility and financial stability. Investing in future generations' educational ambitions gives them more than simply a financial advantage; it also provides them with the information, skills, and chances they need to prosper and contribute meaningfully to society.

Establishing Educational Funds:

There are many methods to provide educational money for your beneficiaries:

- 529 schemes: These tax-favored college savings schemes provide major advantages. Contributions grow tax-free and may be withdrawn tax-free for eligible school costs.
- UTMA/UGMA Accounts: With these custodial accounts, you may donate money or investments to a child for educational reasons. While these accounts provide certain tax advantages, ownership is transferred to the recipient when they reach adulthood, regardless of financial maturity.

Additional considerations:

- Matching Funds: Some educational institutions have matching programs that will double or treble your original donations, considerably increasing the effect of your donation.
- Scholarships and Grants: Consider creating scholarships or grants in your community or alma mater to help kids from underprivileged backgrounds, so continuing your legacy of educational opportunity.

Family businesses: fostering legacy and collaboration

Family enterprises may be an effective strategy to create and keep wealth across generations. They provide special advantages:

- Shared Values and Vision: Family companies are often founded on shared values and a same vision,

which encourages teamwork and long-term commitment.
- Entrepreneurial Spirit: You may inculcate the entrepreneurial spirit in future generations, empowering them to carry on the family tradition.

Challenges and considerations:

- Succession Planning: Creating a clear succession plan is critical to ensuring a seamless transfer of leadership and ownership.
- Family Dynamics: Effective communication and conflict resolution skills are essential for maintaining family peace and preventing division.

Charitable Giving: Leaving a Lasting Impact on the World

Charitable giving is an effective approach to extend your legacy beyond your immediate family and make a positive difference for a subject you care about. There are many methods to include charity contributions in your legacy plan:

- Direct Donations: You may designate a part of your inheritance to go to a certain charity.
- Charitable Trusts: Several kinds of trusts, including charitable remainder trusts (CRTs) and charitable lead trusts (CLTs), provide tax breaks while benefiting your chosen charity.

Building a Legacy of Social Responsibility

By include charitable giving in your legacy plan, you not only assist worthwhile organizations but also set an example for future generations to embrace philanthropy and social responsibility.

Intangible assets: Values and Life Lessons

While financial assets are crucial, accumulating generational wealth goes beyond the tangible. Consider the ideals you want to pass on to future generations. This might include work ethic, resilience, kindness, and a strong moral compass.

- Family customs: Maintaining family customs and rituals fosters long-lasting memories and develops generational relationships.
- Personal experiences and History: Documenting your family history and sharing personal experiences can assist future generations understand and appreciate their ancestry.

Building generational wealth entails making a long-term influence. By embracing tactics other than conventional wealth transfer, you may leave a legacy that goes beyond financial assets. Investing in education, cultivating an entrepreneurial spirit, and supporting causes you believe in may inspire future generations and create a better future for your family and the community. Remember that the most significant legacy you can leave is not money, but a solid foundation of values, knowledge, and a desire to make the world a better place.

Conclusion

You've set out on a mission to create a legacy that will last long beyond your lifetime. This book provides you with the information and resources you need to navigate the world of estate planning, reduce taxes, and empower your loved ones. Remember, creating generational wealth is a marathon, not a sprint. Review your plan on a frequent basis, make adjustments when your circumstances change, and, most importantly, speak freely with your family about your intentions. By promoting financial knowledge, prudent stewardship, and a common vision for the future, you may leave a lasting legacy that will enrich and elevate future generations. So, use what you've learned, enjoy the process, and create a legacy that represents your beliefs and generates a greater future for your family.

www.ingramcontent.com/pod-product-compliance
Lightning Source LLC
Chambersburg PA
CBHW050252230526
45470CB00005B/2222